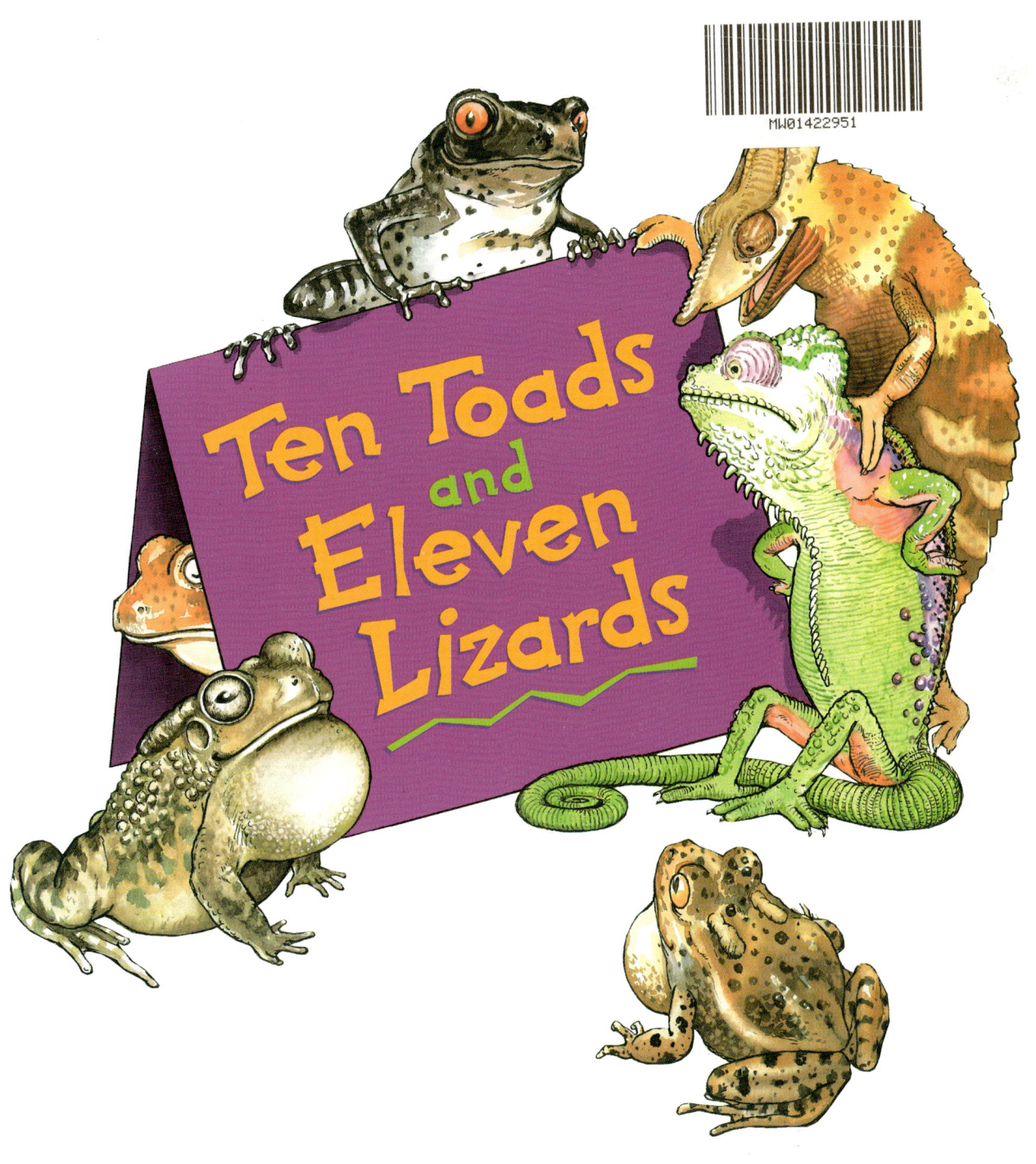

Ten Toads and Eleven Lizards

Written by Cass Hollander ■ Illustrated by Judy Love

MODERN CURRICULUM PRESS

PROJECT DIRECTOR: Susan Cornell Poskanzer   PRODUCT MANAGERS: Christine A. McArtor
             Leslie A. Baranowski   Denise Smith
EXECUTIVE EDITOR: Wendy Whitnah
ART DIRECTOR: Lisa Olsson
DESIGNER: creatives nyc, Inc.

Published by Modern Curriculum Press

MODERN CURRICULUM PRESS
A Division of Pearson Learning
299 Jefferson Road, Parsippany, NJ 07054
800-321-3106 / mcschool.com

Copyright © 1994 by McClanahan Book Company, Inc. All rights reserved.

Manufactured in the United States of America. This book or parts thereof may not be reproduced in any form or mechanically stored in any retrieval system without written permission of the publisher.

This edition is published simultaneously in Canada by Globe/Modern Curriculum Press, Toronto.

ISBN 0-8136-1347-7 (STY PK)   ISBN 0-8136-1348-5 (BB)   ISBN 0-8136-1349-3 (SB)

7 8 9 10   04 03 02 01 00

Our teacher had a little surprise for us.

There were ten toads and eleven lizards!

And they all got loose!

We found three toads under the table and two lizards on top of the books.

Then there were three toads and two lizards.

We found two toads by the fish tank and two lizards on the wall.

Then there were five toads and four lizards.

We found two toads in the toy box and a lizard on Betty Lee's leg!

Then there were seven toads and five lizards.

We found two toads in a locker and three lizards on a lunch box.

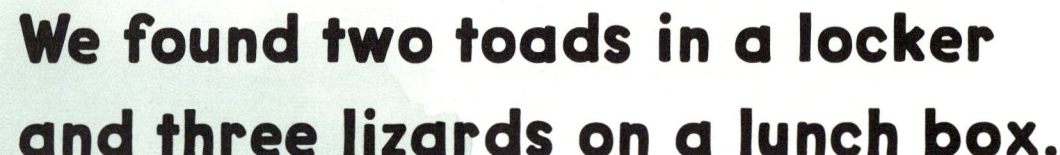

Then there were nine toads and eight lizards.

We found two toads on the window ledge and three lizards in the plants.

Then there were eleven toads and eleven lizards.

What? Eleven toads?